Paper Engineer

by Isabel Thomas

What Does a Paper Engineer Do?

An engineer is a person who designs and makes things. Engineers use lots of different things.

Paper engineers design and make things from paper and card.

An engineer made this incredible model from paper.

How Does a Paper Engineer Work?

Paper is easy to cut. Fold and join it to make new things. You can be a paper engineer, too. Start by learning some paper engineering tricks.

Use templates

Print or **trace** a shape onto card. Cut it out. Place this card template on paper. Then draw around it to copy the shape.

Use scrap paper and card

Raid the **recycling** box for scrap paper and card. Use interesting shapes in your **designs**.

Experiment without cutting

Try tearing, twisting and scrunching paper instead of cutting it. What **textures** can you create?

Work with a helper.

Engineer a Rocket

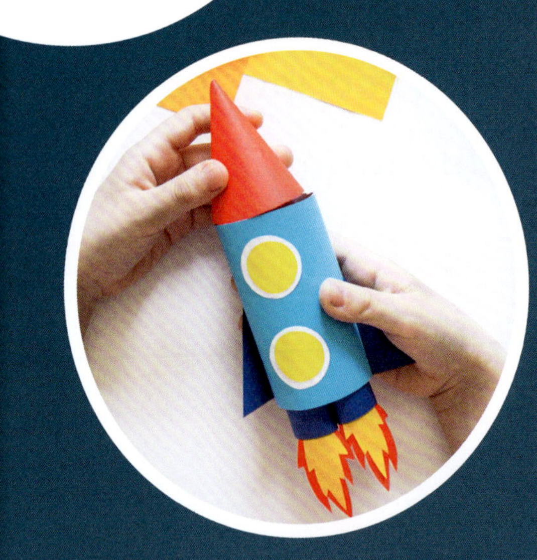

Gather these things:

- paper
- pencil
- glue
- card tube

Step by step

1) Wrap the card tube in paper.

2) Roll two small paper tubes. Push them into the bottom of the card tube. These will make your rocket boosters.

3 Stick on paper circles to make windows.

4 Add red and yellow paper to make the blaze trail.

5 Use paper triangles to make fins.

6 Roll up a paper semicircle to make a cone. Glue the cone to the top of your rocket.

Blast off!

Engineer a Spinning Wheel

Gather these things:

- large paper square
- ruler
- pencil
- glue
- thin stick
- pin

Step by step

1 Draw a line from corner 1 to corner 3. Then draw a line from corner 2 to corner 4.

2 Cut along each line. Do not cut all the way to the middle.

3 Fold corner 4 into the middle of the square. Stick it down.

4 Fold corners 3, 2 and 1 into the middle of the square. Stick them down.

You could **decorate** your finished spinning wheel.

5 Pin your wheel to a thin stick and make it spin!

Make lots of wheels and display them!

Engineer a Sunflower

Gather these things:

- yellow paper
- black tissue paper
- card
- glue

Step by step

1. Trace a petal shape. Cut it out of card to make a template.

2. Use your template to cut out 13 yellow petals.

It is important to cut out the petals carefully.

3 Curl the petals like this.

4 Glue the petals to a circle to make a flower.

5 Scrunch up pieces of dark tissue paper into little balls.

6 Glue the balls in the middle of your flower.

Engineer a Fox

Gather these things:

- sheet of paper
- black felt tip

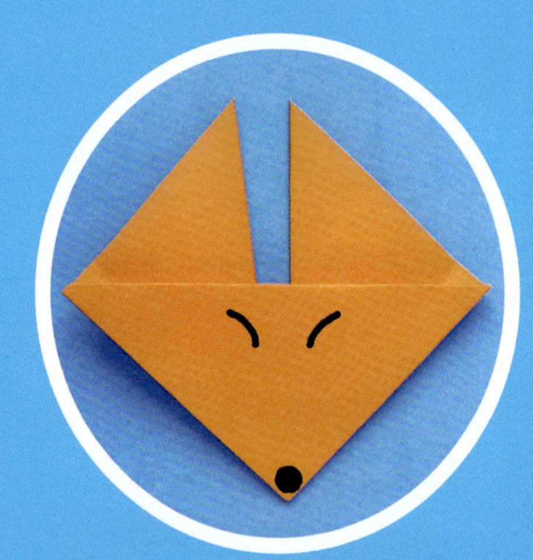

1 Fold the paper in half.

2 Fold the point down to meet the bottom.

3 Fold the right hand point so it sticks up.

4 Fold the left hand point so it sticks up.

5 Turn the paper over.

6 Draw a face.

Have fun making more paper designs!

Glossary

decorate: to make something look nicer

designs: plans of how to make something

experiment: to have a go at something, without knowing if it will work

recycling: to change something into something different

textures: the way that different things feel

trace: to copy a picture onto special transparent paper

Index